Funtastic Fall

Creative Clip Art for Classroom, Home, and Teacher Resource

Created & Designed by Dianne J. Hook

© 2004, Carson-Dellosa Publishing Company, Inc., Greensboro, North Carolina 27425. Illustrations © Dianne J. Hook, PO Box 467, Coalville, Utah 84017. The purchase of this material entitles the buyer to reproduce pages for classroom and home use only. Reproduction of any illustrations in this publication for commercial use is strictly prohibited. Reproduction of these materials for an entire school or district is prohibited. No part of this book may be reproduced (except as noted above), stored in a retrieval system, or transmitted in any form or by any means (mechanically, electronically, recording, etc.) without the prior written consent of Carson-Dellosa Publishing Company, Inc. and Dianne J. Hook.

ISBN:1-59441-006-2

Contents

Credits

Illustrator: Dianne J. Hook
Content Design and Project Director: Sherrill B. Flora
Editor: Karen Seberg
Production: Mark Conrad
Cover Production: Annette Hollister-Papp

Clip Art Assembly Basics

Here are some suggestions as you make your flyers,
announcements, or any project using clip art from this book.

Tools

Putting together the right tools will make your project go more smoothly and look better in the end. A good **copy machine** is a must. It's worth the extra effort to make sure your school or copy shop has machines that make clean copies. You will also need a bottle of white **paper correction fluid**, a fine-tip **black marker** to combine designs and add your own art to the project, **rubber cement** to mount the design onto your paper during the layout stage of your project, and **scissors** for cutting apart the designs you choose. Optional tools to help create a professional-looking project are a **nonreproducible blue pencil**, to make marks that will not show up on copies, a **proportion scale**, to help you determine the size of the reduction or enlargement necessary to fit your paper, and **blue grid paper** for laying out the project with straight lines.

Assembly Steps

1. Choose the design or designs you will be putting together for the project that you will be making.

2. Copy the design once from the book so that you have a copy from which to work without having to cut apart your book.

3. Cut out the designs from your copy and lay them out on your paper. (Blue grid paper comes in handy.) A light table can also help with the layout of your page.

4. Next, make a copy of the designs and any text on the paper before adding any other hand-drawn illustrations. Drawing over the grid paper lines is difficult and generally doesn't turn out well.

5. Now you have a good idea of what your project is going to look like. Go ahead and add all the extra finishing touches. Small doodles or even simple dots or squares can really "warm up" the page and keep it from looking choppy.

6. Make your final copies of the page. Easy!

Hints

- Keep a ¼-inch margin on all edges of your paper.
- If the edges of the cutout pieces are visible on your copies, lighten the copy machine one notch or use correction fluid on one copy and then use it to make the final copies.
- Removable tape is great for creating layouts if you will be using the design more than once.

Have fun! You can become an artist and create wonderful
projects for your class with the help of this book!

Back to School

Welcome

A note from your Teacher

EXTRA...EXTRA!!
Read all about it!

You're at the TOP!

You really MEASURE up!

Noteworthy...

Write On!

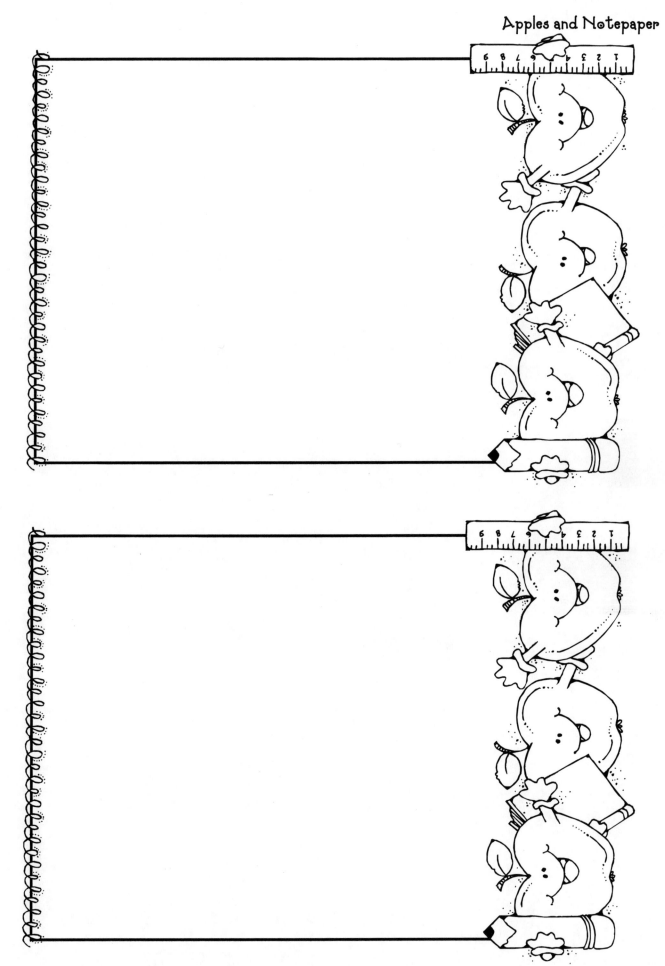

Take Your Pick

Take Your 'PICK!'

13

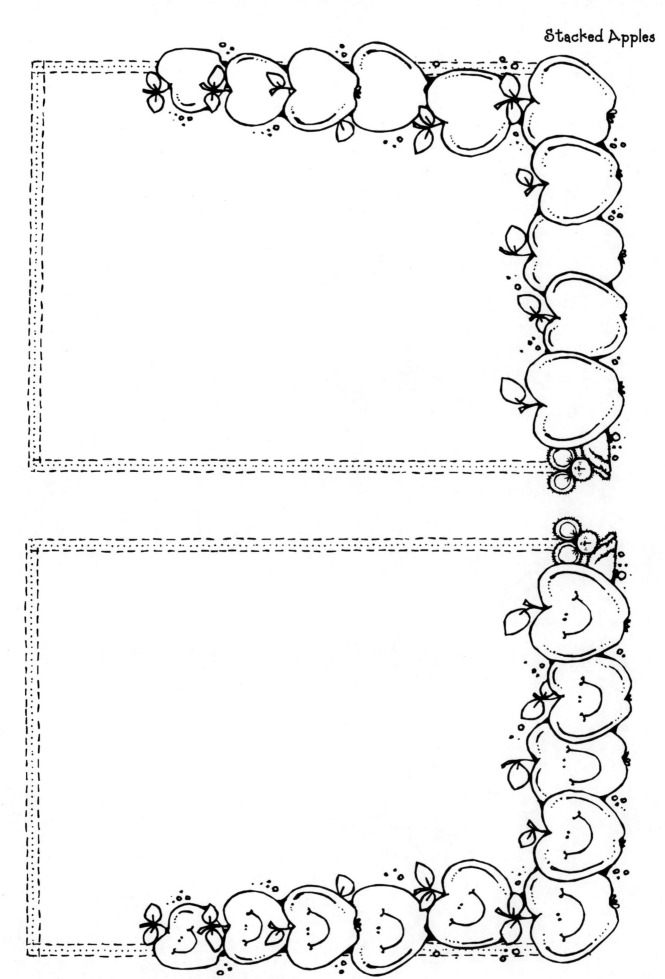

Stacked Apples

All for Fall

SMILE!

SMILE!

SMILE!

Harvest Hank

Autumn

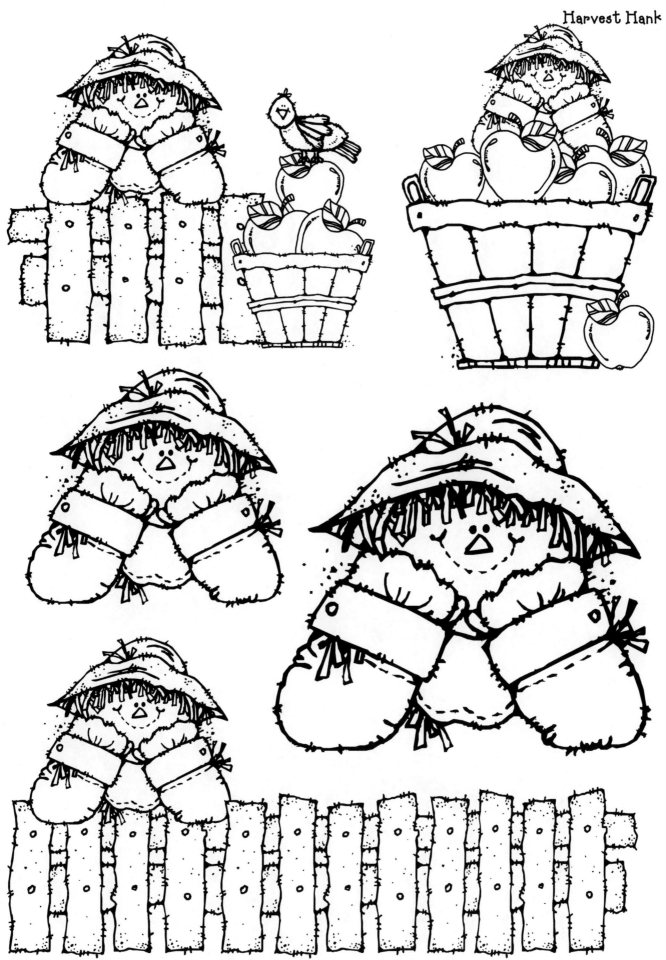

Harvest Hank

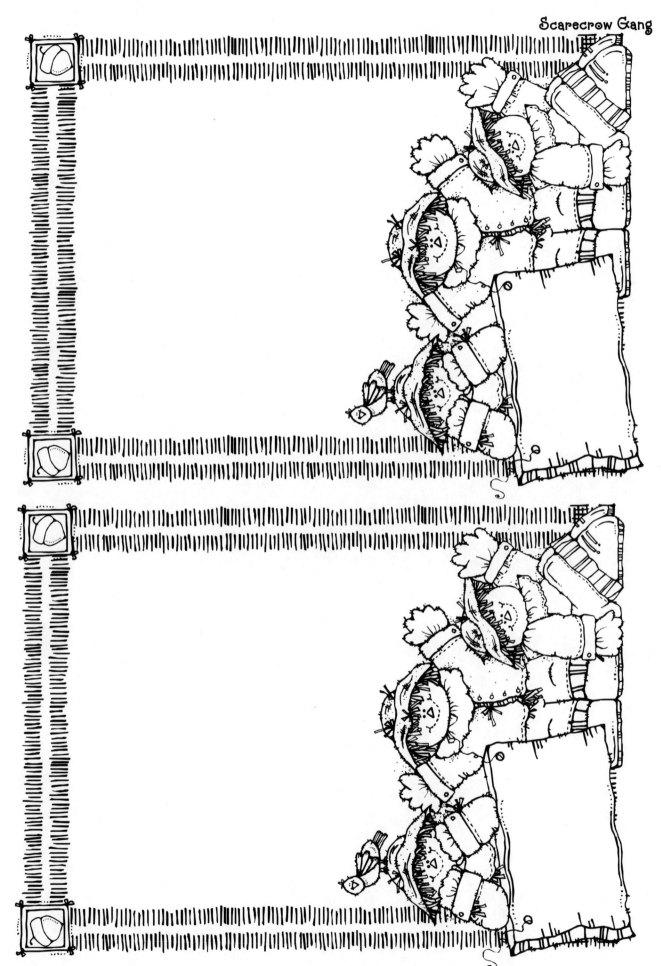

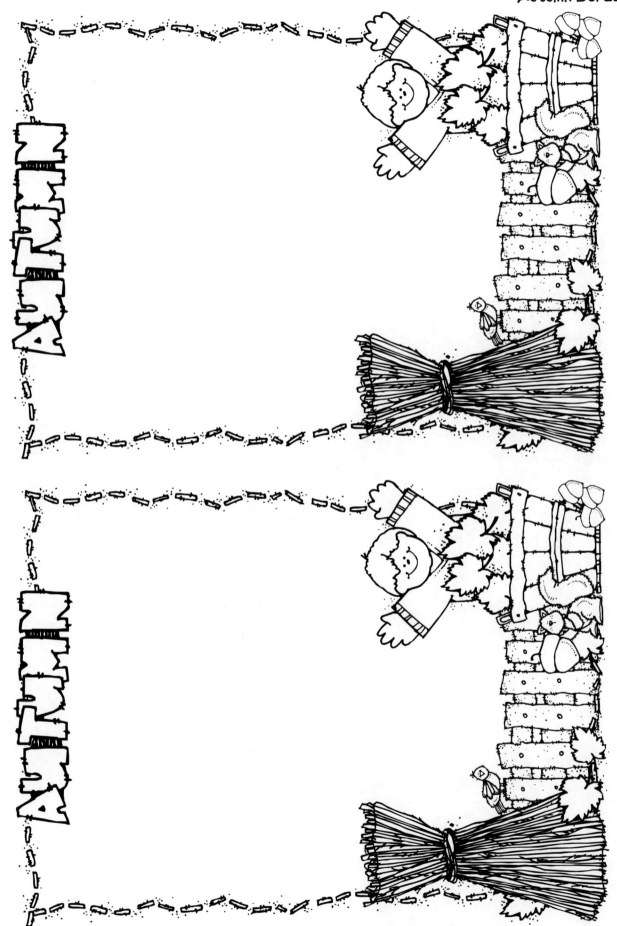

READ

READ

Pumpkin Patch

Pumpkin Patch

Pumpkin Painting

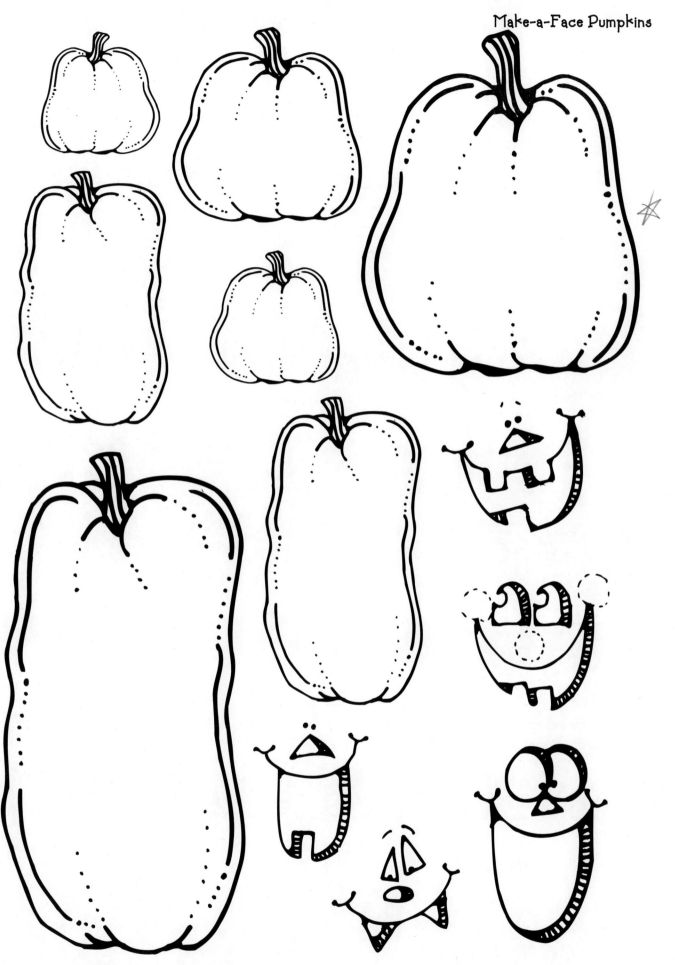

33

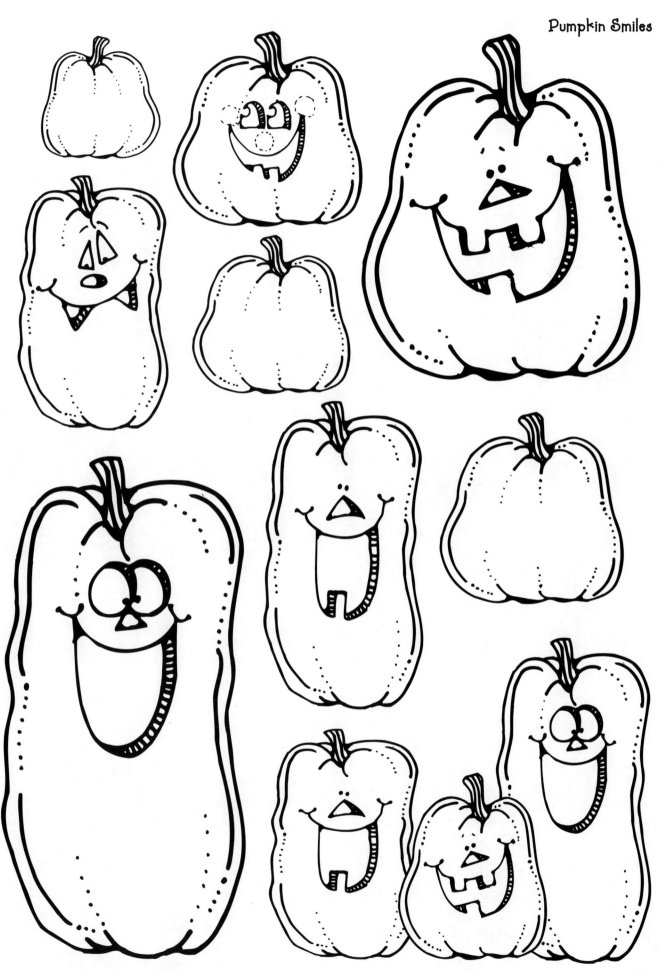

Pumpkin Border

36

Giant Pumpkin Border

Funny Frank

Quite 'FRANK'ly...

Laughing Pumpkins

42

★ October ★

43

44

Spiders and Webs

47

FALL

Let's Eat

53

THANKSGIVING

THANKSGIVING

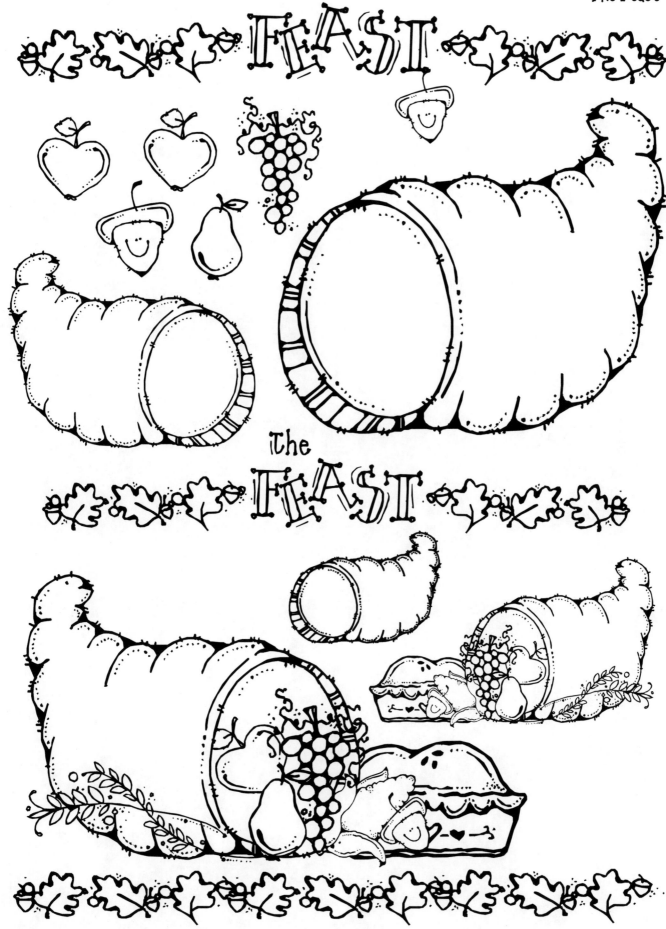

Turkey Time Border

Fall Friends Border

Autumn Mouse Border

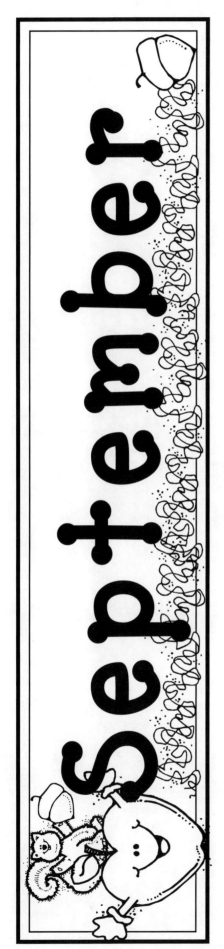

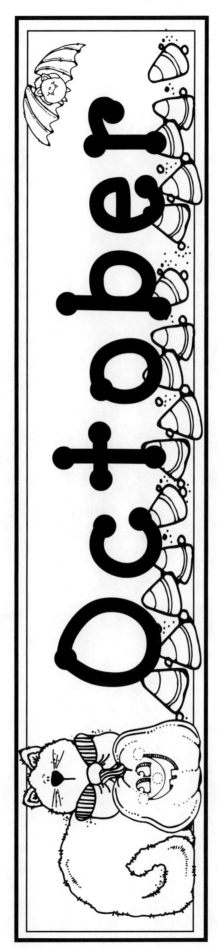

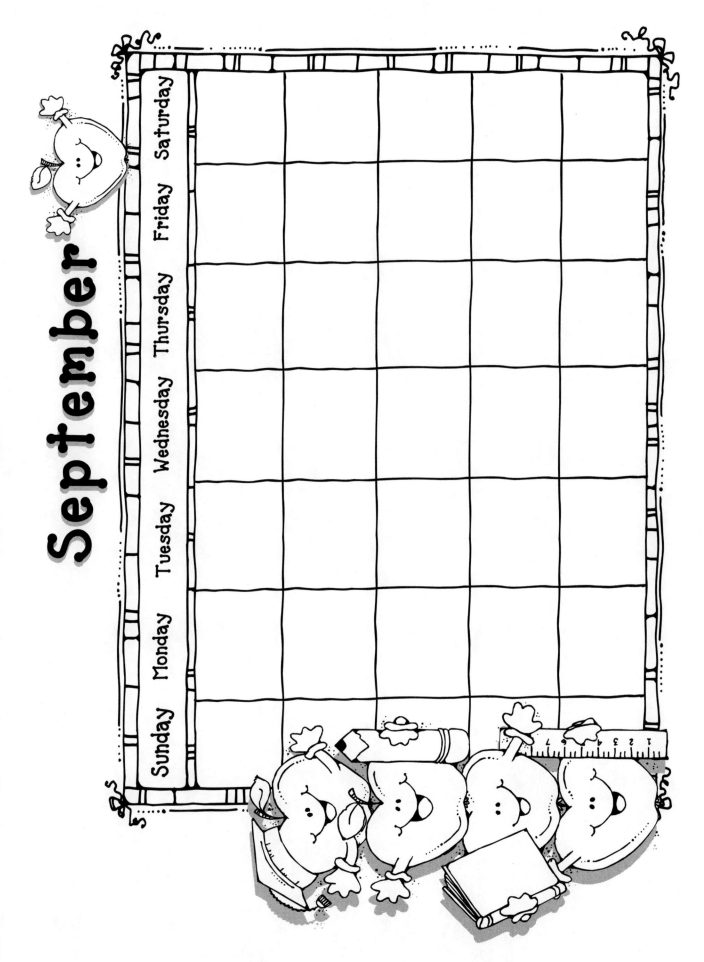

September

Sunday	Monday	Tuesday	Wednesday	Thursday	Friday	Saturday

October

Sunday Monday Tuesday Wednesday Thursday Friday Saturday

Boo to YOU!

November

Sunday Monday Tuesday Wednesday Thursday Friday Saturday